Let's Go Outside is © Flying Eye Books 2015.

This is a first edition published in 2015 by Flying Eye Books, an imprint of
Nobrow Ltd. 62 Great Eastern Street, London, EC2A 3QR.

Text and illustrations © Katja Spitzer 2015.
Katja Spitzer has asserted her right under the Copyright, Designs and Patents Act,
1988, to be identified as the Author of this Work.

Published in the US by Nobrow (US) Inc.

Printed in Poland on FSC assured paper.
ISBN: 978-1-909263-51-2

Order from www.flyingeyebooks.com

Katja Spitzer

LET'S GO
OUTSIDE

Flying Eye Books

London – New York

Flowers

Gardening

Insects

Butterfly

Fruit and vegetables

Bird

Clothes line

The neighbour's cat

Cherries

Tools

Pool

Tree

Swing

Squirrel

Toadstool

Leaves

Pumpkin

Hedgehog

Snowman